T5-AQE-822

JACK KRAMER

The Indoor Gardener's First Aid Book

DRAWINGS BY MICHAEL VALDEZ

PHOTOS BY MATTHEW BARR

SIMON AND SCHUSTER · NEW YORK

DESIGNED BY EVE METZ
MANUFACTURED IN THE UNITED STATES OF AMERICA

1 2 3 4 5 6 7 8 9 10
LIBRARY OF CONGRESS CATALOGING IN PUBLICATION DATA

KRAMER, JACK
    THE INDOOR GARDENER'S FIRST AID BOOK.

    1. HOUSE PLANTS—DISEASES AND PESTS.   I. TITLE.
SB608.H84K7   635.9′65   75-15593
ISBN 0-671-22080-2

Contents

INTRODUCTION: A Healthy Plant Is a Happy One!

Whether they are tiny seedlings you have grown yourself, or plants you have bought, your houseplants are dear to you. You care about them and when they appear wilted or sickly you worry and wonder what to do to help them. Well, *you can help them* if you know what is wrong and how to remedy it. That's what this book is about. It's your handbook for maintaining a healthy, thriving indoor garden, and for saving plants from death and destruction.

Plants *do get sick,* just as you or I might. As time passes, or as more and more plants are introduced into one's collection, so are the chances increased of having to deal with sick plants. Not necessarily because the new plants may be carriers of illness, or that one is neglectful, but simply because of the law of averages—sooner or later *everyone* who grows plants indoors will experience pests or disease in them. It could be a cultural mishap such as not enough or too much water, or it might be an insect or disease attack. The main thrust of this survival kit is to get you to know what to look for and recognize symptoms when plants fail. And then of course, what to do to save them.

Specific remedies are given for creepy crawly things such as mites and aphids. Fungus and bacterial diseases, those nefarious culprits that can ruin plants, are thoroughly discussed. Further, there is information on plants that can take more abuse than others—that may be more problem-free than their cousins.

There is a chapter on specific plants and their specific problems (or non-problems as the case might be). Drawings of insects and diseases you may not want to know have also crept into this volume, not to frighten you but to help you to know what to look for on plants.

The Indoor Gardener's First Aid Book was written to help you help your indoor plants. With this book in hand there is no reason why your plants should sniffle or shrivel, moan or groan, or swoon in despair. Remember that a healthy plant is a happy one!

JACK KRAMER

The
Indoor Gardener's
First Aid Book

Insect-free plants are beautiful plants; here is a healthy group: Dracaena wernecki (bottom left), Calathea (left), Corn plant (center), Ananus cosmosus (Bromeliad, at top) and Cissus (grape ivy, at right).

1 · Knowing Your Plants

WE ALL WANT healthy, attractive-looking green plants;
none of us want sick ones. Watching a plant grow and
prosper is part of the pleasure of having houseplants, but
ailing plants are always a disappointment, and sometimes
a costly one at that. A great many problems with plants
start with the wrong cultural care—too much water kills
more plants than any other one thing—but there are
other problems that can occur too, namely: chewing and
sucking insects, fungus and bacteria diseases, and virus
infections. If you have any kind of collection of houseplants and want to keep them beautiful, it is essential
that you learn about the things that can harm your
plants. That way, you can diagnose problems at the
earliest possible stage.

Insects are serious considerations with houseplants,
but injuries also affect plants. Fern fronds striking the
glass turn brown; leaves that are frequently bruised by

handling wither, and there are always accidents—plants fall and stems break. You can master all these problems (and save almost any plant) with a little know-how.

Outdoors, if plant become sickly, many will naturally recover because various elements are at work in the soil and the air. Predatory insects and birds kill bug infestations before they can take over. Indoors we have no such allies—and must be as responsible to our plants as to our pets, willing to devote some time to them. In your home, houseplants are at your mercy and you must be Mother Nature, so put on your crown and go to work. Learning her tricks is not easy, but it isn't impossible. And it isn't a matter of having magic healing powers, or playing guessing games. The more regular detective work that is done, observing plants and looking for clues, the less chance of invasion and disease. If you do save a plant and feel a bit smug about it, enjoy it—you've helped a living thing, and both you and the plant will feel better about it!

Cultural Checklists

It's not my intention here to cover all aspects of plant care and culture. In fact, I am assuming that you have some basic knowledge of what your plants require in the way of soil mixes, watering, feeding, potting and light situations. Every indoor gardener should invest in at least one basic book that covers plant care and culture in detail. I recommend, also, that you consider taking a short course on indoor plants—more and more garden clubs, botanic gardens and adult education centers at local high schools are offering these, and if you are fortunate enough to find such a course available in your city or

A well-grown iron-cross Begonia is a beautiful sight to see; this plant unfortunately is not as attractive as it should be, because leaves have been bruised and eaten at edges by insects and stems are limp.

town, it's fun to join and well worth the fees involved.

What follows are quick checklists of do's and don'ts that most beginners tend to overlook.

SOILS

To start with, learn about soils. Some plants will grow in any soil, but most won't. Remember that since your plants are confined to soil in the container, soil should be fertile and full of nutrients. In a year's time (sometimes less), plants deplete the soil of nutrients and must have additional feeding. Plant foods are available, but often too much feeding can harm plants, so yearly repotting in fresh soil is necessary. Sounds like a lot to keep in mind? It is, so be prepared. Here's a rundown on soils:

Packaged soils (general houseplant kind) are fine for all plants, but do add some sand—$\frac{1}{3}$ sand to $\frac{2}{3}$ soil—for cacti and succulents and for other plants some compost or manure (follow directions on packets).

Avoid soilless mixes. These have no nutrients, and feeding is necessary all the time. Quite a bother!

Soil bought by the bushel from a nursery is already mixed and has all necessary nutrients; it's the best you can get.

Don't wet soil before using; keep it dry or you'll end up a muddy mess (you, not the plant).

Don't skimp on soil. Pack it down firmly (but not tightly) in the container.

Do add charcoal chips to the soil to keep it sweet and to avoid lots of problems. (Use some from your fireplace, or buy aquarium charcoal.)

Don't add earthworms to indoor soils; you'll only have wormy soil, not a better plant.

Always use sterilized soil. This should be specified on all packaged soils.

This Calathea is not suffering from insect damage; the leaves are curled because it is not getting enough soil nutrients.

FEEDING

You'll also have to know something about plant foods to keep your plants healthy. You must know what they can and can't do for the plants. Some plants, such as ferns and palms, cannot tolerate and absorb feeding. Excess feeding can also cause a buildup of toxic salts that can harm plants. Here's a checklist of plant foods:

There are granular, soluble, and foliar foods. Use the granular pellets because they're easy to put on soil; then water.

Never feed an ailing plant. It doesn't need it, and it can't take it.

Never feed a plant in its rest cycle (generally in winter).

Never try to force a plant into growth with excessive feedings. It won't work; you'll kill the plant.

Don't worry about all those numbers on the feeding packages; use 10–10–5 for everything. It's fine.

Do add some fish emulsion once every few months. Yes, it smells fishy but it's darn good stuff for most plants. Mix with water as indicated on the container.

Add some bone meal to plants, especially flowering ones when you pot them. Use one tablespoon to a 6-inch pot.

Don't try to make an organic compost for your houseplants. Making dinner is usually enough trouble, let alone mixing garbage.

CONTAINERS

Although soil and plant foods are important, containers are also part of the good houseplant picture. Avoid containers that don't have drainage because sufficient drainage is essential for plants' good health. Plastic pots hold water longer than clay pots; this can affect some plants as plants in clay pots need water more frequently. Wood containers allow water to evaporate slowly, but this can sometimes contribute to fungus growth. The size of the pot is important. A pot too large for a plant's root system leaves an excess amount of unused soil that if

This Geranium in a novelty container is not doing well: leaves are limp and plant is ill-formed. The problem is probably that the container does not have drainage holes, and excess water has turned soil sour at the bottom of the pot.

too wet can get soggy and affect the plant badly. On the other hand, a container too small for a plant can cause thwarted growth. A general rule is to allow an inch or so of soil around the root system of a newly potted plant. When you get a new plant home, knock it gently out of the pot to see that it is neither pot bound, nor too roomy in the soil.

WATERING

The quality of the water you use for plants has been under much discussion lately, but this is unimportant. If you can drink the water, you can use it for plants. Whether it's alkaline or acidic makes little difference to houseplants, although it does make a difference outdoors.

Exact quantities for watering plants are usually superfluous, such as keep this one dry, that one moist, the other barely moist. Certain plants do have specific requirements, but generally and almost without exception, if all cultural conditions are good, plants should be watered thoroughly in summer and even in winter, especially if artificial heating is high. If in doubt, underwater rather than overwater. Soak plants thoroughly, until water drains out from the bottom of the pot, and everyone will be happy. Don't worry about the time of day to water plants. Most sources say morning, but it doesn't really make any difference. Here's a quick rundown on watering plants:

Base your watering schedule on how dry the soil feels to the touch, and when it is dry, water thoroughly.

Try to use room-temperature water (let it stand overnight).

When plants are actively growing, give them more water than when they're resting.

Plants in clay pots need a more frequent watering schedule than those in plastic pots as the plastic pots hold the water longer.

Water newly planted specimens sparsely for the first few weeks.

Once a month, if possible, soak pots to the rim in the tub or sink to eliminate excess salts. Use tepid water and soak for an hour or so or until you see air bubbles on top.

Regular misting and spraying plants—on the top and undersides of leaves—will help prevent insects.

Avoid misting leaves (especially hairy-leaved plants) when sun is shining on them.

When you do mist or spray leaves, use tepid water. Cold water can shock plants and discolor leaves.

Use a really good watering can with a long, no-drip spout.

GRAB BAG OF TIPS

In houseplant culture there are certain basic things you should know. They may seem incidental, but all things contribute to a healthy plant, and a healthy plant is rarely troubled with disease or insects. One of the first things is to try and determine where a plant comes from. This isn't as difficult as it sounds, and indeed is well worth the effort because the native habitat of a plant tells you a good deal about how to keep it healthy. A book called *Hortus,* L. H. Bailey and Ethel Zoe Bailey, Macmillan Co., gives the country of origin of most plants.

Don't worry about where to put plants in the home—bedroom, kitchen and bath are all fine places as long as there is proper lighting. Try them in other locations after they have been in your home for a few weeks, if they seem unhappy.

Don't panic if some plants droop when you get them home from the florist or plant shop. This is normal.

Be aware of drafts. A Dieffenbachia can wilt overnight if left near a hot-air register or an air-conditioning duct. (A Philodendron won't, by the way.) Seasonal houseplants (often called gift plants, for example, Poinsettia, Gloxinia, and Kalanchoe) need special attention.

Don't worry about temperature, but keep your home on the cool side; it's good for you and your plants too. Generally a 10-degree drop at night, which is common in most apartments and homes, is fine for plants.

Do not purchase plants from dubious suppliers, and avoid buying plants in bad health. They should appear strong, green and attractive.

Don't worry too much about exact light conditions. Most plants can adapt to bright light or a shady location. Too much full sun will burn plants, but not enough light won't kill them. They may not live as happily, but they'll survive. So don't be running around the house with a light meter measuring light readings at windows. It will give you exercise, that's about all.

Do turn plants occasionally so all parts get light, and once in a while clip and prune houseplants to keep them trained and pretty. Yes, clip and trim! It won't harm plants; it will encourage new growth. I recently cut down a new houseplant (Pseudopanax) to within 4 inches of the stems because I didn't like the shape. The plant recovered beautifully, and now I'm training it to tree form, which is what I want.

Don't be misled into thinking you have to be a taxonomist or biologist to keep plants healthy. True, there are very technical terms for bacterial fungus and viral infections and so forth. If you can, remember the terms; if not, do the best you can.

2 · *Recognizing the Symptoms*

WITH VERY FEW EXCEPTIONS (virus being one), plants just don't topple over and throw up their hands overnight. Before they become mortally ill they always show symptoms—clues that they're failing and may be on the way to a serious illness, whether it be culture- or insect-caused. Thus, observation is your first line of defense. Watch plants: leaves where trouble may start, stems where trouble often starts, and flowers and buds. Yellow or streaked leaves are definitely a symptom of something amiss, as are soft and brown stems. And foliage that just falls off is certainly an indication of something awry (unless plants are going into rest).

Good culture is of course the best way to avoid plant troubles, and so is catching the trouble before it really gets a foothold. There is absolutely no pest or disease you can't thwart if you catch it before it really becomes serious. Keeping plants well-groomed is another vital part

At first glance (even to the experienced gardener) this plant may seem lost forever. Not so. It is Cyanotis and naturally goes into complete dormancy in winter. In back of plant, new shoots are starting to sprout. Before you decide that it's insects or ill care, be sure plant is not simply resting as this one is.

Mealybug is well in evidence on this Cissus. Plants with infestations as severe as this need immediate care to survive.

of keeping them healthy. Spraying and misting leaves with tepid water—and even occasionally giving leaves a sponge bath—goes a long way in preventing insect infestations, because cleansing tends to remove insect eggs before they hatch.

Sometimes the decline of the plant is caused by improper culture, so before you raise your hands in panic over insects, look to culture. If culture is good and plants still fail, then consider the crawlers. Remember that falling leaves and premature bud drop aren't necessarily caused by insects or disease.

One last, often overlooked, point. Learn about the natural life span of your plants. Some plants will last for years and years; others reach the end of the road in a year or two. So don't be alarmed when the time comes; simply make cuttings of the old plant, take a deep breath and dispose of it. The cuttings can be rooted successfully and you will start anew with the joy of keeping a favorite plant in your collection.

Leaves

A plant's leaves give many clues as to its condition. A clean healthy plant naturally has perky, fresh, green, good-looking foliage, never discolored and streaked. Here are some unhealthy leaf conditions and their probable causes:

Leaf Symptoms	Possible Causes
Brown or yellow areas, bleached yellow areas	Incorrect feeding; sun scorch or mites
Yellow or white spots	Leaf spot disease

Leaf symptoms (*cont.*)	Possible Causes (*cont.*)
Leaf drop	Thrips, mites or overwatering
Brown edges	Anthracnose disease, overwatering, salt damage
Curled	Salt damage, thrips or mites
Dried and brown	Underwatering; not enough nutrients in soil
Smaller leaves than mature ones	Lack of nutrients
Sticky substance	Insects, usually aphids or mealybugs
Silver streaks	Thrips
Eaten at edges	Slugs, snails
Coated white	Mildew and molds
Gray or yellow	Underfertilizing; mold
Deformed	Salt damage, mites
Transparent areas	Thrips

A snail or many snails have had breakfast, lunch, and dinner on this Orchid, and the plant is almost completely eaten. Such a plant should be discarded.

Bacterial rot has attacked leaves of this lipstick vine (Aeschynanthus). It is almost beyond saving, but infected areas can be cut back and dusted with fungicides. Then you hope for the best.

Stems and Crowns

Many fungus diseases start at the crown of the plant, but if caught quickly they can be remedied. If left, the disease can kill the plant. Also, many insects start their colonies in stems and leaf axils, so these are places to really inspect closely. Stems should be healthy and firm

with good color; crowns of plants should be solid, never
turgid or soft.

Stem and Crown Symptoms	Possible Causes
White or powdery stems	Mildew, molds
Limp stems	Overwatering, poor drainage
Stems covered with sugar substance	Ants gathering colonies of aphids
Stems don't develop	Underfeeding or lack of water
Soft stem growth	Crown and stem rot disease, overwatering
Soft crowns	Crown and stem rot disease, overwatering; too much humidity
Brown or gray crowns	Rot, disease; too much humidity, water

Flowers and Buds

Foliage plants are lovely, but more and more people
like the additional challenge of growing flowering species
such as African violets, Geraniums, and Orchids. These
people nurture their plants carefully, until finally buds
appear. But, alas, many times when successful bloom
seems just around the corner, buds drop off or flowers
last but a day. Is something awry? You bet it is. To save
your flowering gems and enjoy their beauty, look to the
following hints:

Flower and Bud Symptoms	Possible Causes
Buds drop off	Low humidity, temperature fluctuation
Buds fail to open	Thrips
Malformed buds	Thrips
Flowers develop spots	Virus
Flowers don't open fully	Day length
Ill-shaped flowers	Mites, virus

Mealybugs have done their work well here. In addition, snails have joined the feast, as evidenced in eaten leaf edges.

Scale is easily seen on this spider plant (Chlorophytum), but as yet no lethal damage. Stop insects quickly and plants can be saved.

Overwatering and high humidity have caused bacterial disease on edges of leaves in the furry-leaved Siderasis. Cut away infected areas to save plant.

For specific insects and diseases and their descriptions, and plants most affected, see Chapters 3, 4. Controls are also discussed there.

If It's Pest or Disease

Sometimes, even with the best of culture, plants will be attacked by insects or disease. If you discover a light insect attack, there's little chance that you'll lose the plant. It can be saved by a chemical spray or by old-fashioned remedies such as laundry–soap-and-water spray. The main thing, however, is to know what you're fighting before you do battle. Most common houseplant insects are recognizable on sight, or if you're wearing bifocals, they're identifiable with a magnifying glass. This includes the pesky aphids, the insidious spider mites, the icky mealybugs, and the rather fascinating insect called scale. Lesser pests such as snails are known all too well on sight, as are slugs. If, however, the bug doesn't fall into the descriptions in the next chapter's listings, pick off the culprit (dead, that is) and mail it to your County Agricultural Agency. They may be able to identify it and help. (You shouldn't have to do this, because we cover a great many insects, but I want you to have all bases covered, just in case.)

In summary, follow this line of detective work to determine what is ailing a plant:

1. Is the plant getting too much or not enough water?

2. Is the plant being overfed?

3. Is the plant getting too much heat?

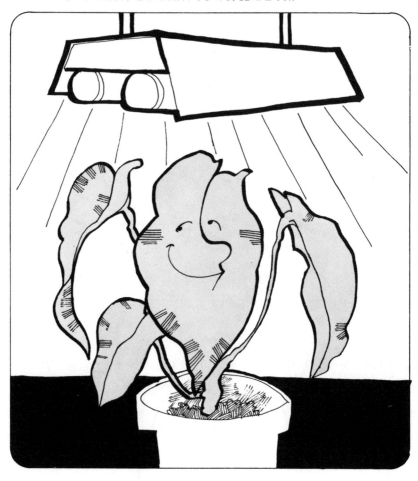

4. Is the plant getting enough light?

5. Are there insects invading the plant?

3 · *Know the Invaders*

"KNOWING IS GROWING" is a phrase often used in garden books. Knowing how to care for plants certainly is important, but knowing how to protect them against insects and disease is more important. No matter how well you take care of a plant, if insects or disease attack it, it can wither and die. But just as there are many bugs and bacteria that can attack people, so too there are several kinds of insects and diseases that attack plants. None, if caught early, are fatal. However, to prevent any fatalities you must know what the bug is and what to do about it.

The list of houseplant insects is small; there are only about twelve kinds of bugs that attack indoor plants. So you don't have to be an entomologist to cope. There are chewing insects such as thrips and sucking insects such as aphids and scale, and each insect looks different from the other, so identification (without exception) is vital. Buy a small magnifying glass and inspect your plants with it regularly.

It also helps to know something about an insect's sex life. Yes, their sex life. Once you realize how quickly insects can multiply, you'll see why it's necessary to act fast in administering first aid to a plant. While you are sleeping at night, one healthy mealybug can produce 600 children. Think about that for a nightmare!

Common Insects

Common insects can be controlled without too much trouble. This group includes aphids, mealybugs, scale, red spider, thrips, whiteflies, and ants. Again, none are serious invaders unless you let them go unchecked. Remember the mealybug's breeding habits!

ANTS

There have been stories written about the intelligence of ants. Anything you have seen or read is true. These are frightfully intelligent insects. And if you see them around your plants get ready for trouble. They are not only warriors as evidenced in their fictional stories, they are also in fact herders. Ants gather, take care, and protect colonies of aphids and mealybugs, using the sweet honeydew secreted by these insects as some of their own food and food for their future generations. (Ants, however, do not eat plants.)

If I sound adamant about ants on plants, it is not just because of the rhyme. I am, because I know they can wreak havoc with houseplants and have with mine. The aphid seems stupid by comparison and easily eradicated. Not so with ants. They are difficult to get rid of, and just

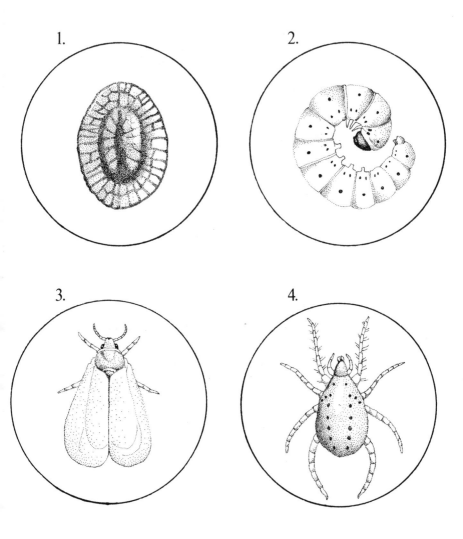

1.

2.

3.

4.

5.

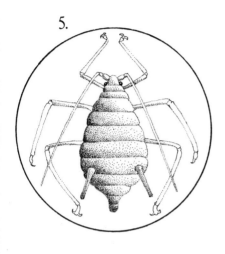

6.

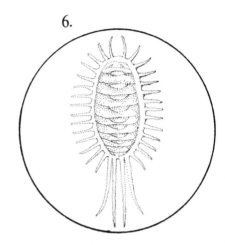

1. SCALE

2. CUTWORM

3. WHITEFLY

4. RED SPIDER MITE

5. APHID

6. MEALYBUG

7. THRIP

7.

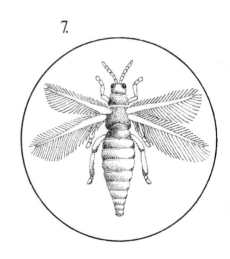

when you think they have gone off to your neighbor's house, they appear with more relatives to plague your plants.

Since there are so many different kinds of ants, it is equally difficult to know what to do to get rid of them. I have seen brown ants and black ones in my kitchen and light brown and dark black ones on my plants. Of course, strong chemicals like Chlordane help keep them away, and although I object to using extreme remedies, when I see a drove of ants I do reach for the Chlordane dust. This will hardly endear me to organic gardeners but there are limits.

APHIDS

Aphids, also known as plant lice, are sucking insects, and there are a variety of them. Generally, however, they are all similar in appearance, and it doesn't really make much difference which one you are fighting. An aphid is an aphid, and there are ways to eliminate them. Aphids, from the family Aphididae, bear live young. In general, aphids hatch in spring. They are viviparous females able to reproduce without fertilization by a male. They hold their young in their body until the proper time; they then drop them in your plant. They produce similar females, some that develop wings (but most aphids are wingless), and these migrate to other plants when a colony becomes crowded. In autumn (another spawning season) male and female wingless aphids are born. These mate, and then we have oviparous females that lay fertilized eggs for overwintering. In warmth, living young can be produced continually, with no overwintering egg stage.

Typical aphids are pear-shaped, small, soft-bodied critters with a beak that has 4 needlelike stylets. Aphids use

APHIDS

these daggers to pierce plant tissue and suck out plant sap. These insects also secrete honeydew or sugar from their butts; this excretion is a great breeding ground for the growth of a black fungus known as sooty mold (discussed in a later chapter).

There's confusion about aphids because rumor says that they're either brown or gray. Not so. Aphids come in a veritable treasure house of colors: black, red, green (quite pretty), pink, yellow, lavender, and gray. Also, the young aphids (nymphs) may differ in color from the adult. They are, of course, much smaller and difficult to see, but there's no need to get alarmed because you must first have mature aphids before you get little ones. Most aphids live their life cycle on one single plant; others are wanderers and eat many different plants.

How do you know if a plant has aphids? First, by looking for them. If you can't see them, watch the plant: *it loses vigor, may become stunted, and leaves may curl or pucker as juices are drained out by the bugs.* Because aphids are also carriers (or vectors) of mosaic and other virus diseases, it's of utmost importance that you get rid of them.

MEALYBUGS

If you've seen cottony accumulations in the leaf axils or on the leaf veins of your plants, you have met mealybugs. These are relatives of scale insects, members of the family Pseudococcidae in the order Hemiptera. Mealybugs have soft, segmented bodies dressed in cotton wax. The adult female deposits her eggs, about 300 to 600 of them, at leaf axils or where stems branch, in a waxy sac from the butt end of her body. In about 10 days the eggs hatch, and the parade starts. The youngsters are crawling, oval-shaped, light yellow, six-legged insects with smooth bodies. They have beaks that they insert into plant parts to get sap to fill their little bellies. *As the sap leaves your plant, your plant wilts.* Once they start feeding, the little mealybugs develop the cottony waxy cover-

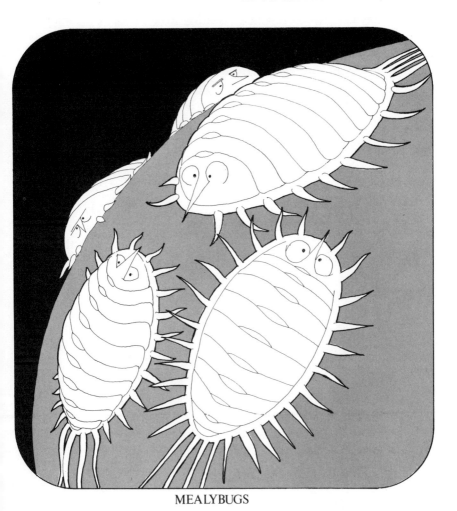

MEALYBUGS

ing. They move slower and slower as days go by, but they don't really stop moving, although you may not be able to discern this. Like aphids, mealybugs produce a copious honeydew, which forms a breeding ground for sooty mold fungi and attracts ants.

Male mealybugs, unlike the females, develop wings like a fly. Soon after they mate with the female they die. Some mealybugs can become quite large. I've seen some that were ⅛ inch in diameter, which is certainly visible to the naked eye. When mealybugs are this large, it's thus easy to arrest their spreading before they get a foothold.

RED SPIDER MITES

There are mites and there are mites—all kinds. Some are injurious to animals, human beings, and plants. Ironically, mites are not true insects; they're from the animal class Arachnids, and are related to spiders, ticks, and scorpions. The mites have 4 pairs of legs instead of the insects' 3 pairs. They have no antennae or jaws. The true red spider mite that attacks plants is from the family Tetranychidae. These tiny oval creatures may be yellow, green, red, or brown. They have long legs and are almost impossible to see on a plant, but they do spin webs, which often gives them away. Use a magnifying glass and a strong light to look for the webs, and inspect the underside of each leaf for the tiny mite.

Of the many species that attack plants, the two-spotted mite is the worst offender. It isn't particular as to what kind of plant it dines on. Spider mite eggs hatch in 2 or 3 days, in temperatures of 75° F, or after 21 days if temperatures are low (55° F). One female lays a few eggs every day and a total of 100 to 200 eggs during an average life span of 1 month. Thus in 2 weeks, mites' population on a plant can be compared to the people population of, say Chicago.

Mites injure plants by piercing the leaves and sucking

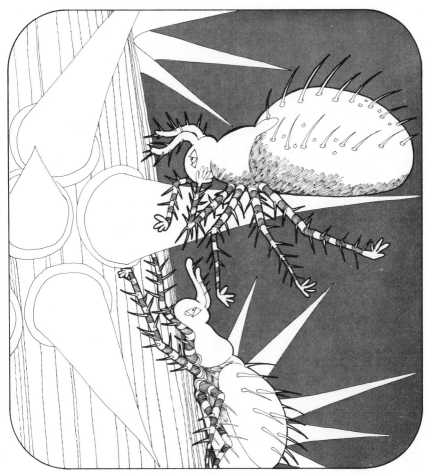

RED SPIDER MITES

out liquid content from the cells. *Foliage turns pale and may become stippled around the injured parts.* New foliage is often smaller than normal, or deformed, and the growth rate of your plant is slower than usual. *If the in-*

festation goes unheeded, the leaves either drop off or be-come rust-red and die. The plants may become covered with silken webs that the mites make as they move from area to area.

Because spider mites are so tiny, they're difficult to see and thus hard to eliminate. Also, their rapid reproduction and habit of using lower leaf surfaces (where you aren't apt to look) as their breeding places make them particu-larly hard to find.

Mites have a well-protected respiratory system, so they're quite resistant to many insecticides, sprays and fumigants; this is especially true when the mites are in their quiescent period.

SCALE

Can you imagine a small armored tank? Well, scale in-sects are somewhat similar: tiny and oval (but can be seen), with an armored shell or scales covering their body. These funsters belong to the family Coccidae and are a very large group of plant violators. The wingless females are mostly responsible for the injury to plants. Scale have a short crawling period (when they have six legs), but once settled on a plant they insert their mouth parts through a leaf and start taking in sap. Female scale insects stay in the same spot throughout their lives, molt-ing twice and laying eggs, in many cases giving birth to live young. The males have an elongated body and even-tually develop wings, thus resembling gnats. They may attack leaves, but they're also fond of stems. *Plants with scale insects show leaf as well as stem damage.*

Of all the insects mentioned, scale is easiest to combat because it's so easily recognizable. Hard scales are the most common, but there are also soft-scale types that at-

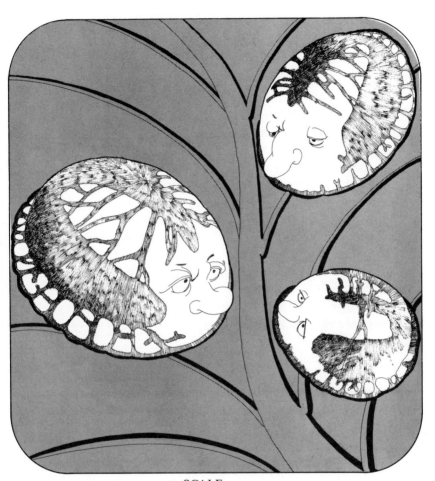

SCALE

tack plants. The insects appear in many different colors and are generally attracted to new rather than mature growth. Either way, scale are highly injurious and should be eliminated quickly.

THRIPS

These are chewing, very small, slender insects with 2 pairs of long narrow wings. The mouth is fitted with "tools" that enable them to pierce or rasp leaves. Most thrips belong to the suborder Terebrantia in the larger order of Thysanoptera. Adults are generally dark in color and most active between spring and summer. The female deposits eggs on stems or in the tissue of plants. The transparent larvae hatch within 2 to 30 days, depending upon the species, and start sucking plant sap. (Be alert and get them early.) After a few days they change their skins and become tougher. Some thrips are carnivorous and attack other thrips, and if the good ones overwhelm the bad ones, you can just sit back and watch the battle. Unfortunately, usually the bad ones win. Some thrips are active flyers, others just sort of jump around, and still others don't move much at all. Thrips are indicated *by silver sheen among the leaves.*

THRIP

WHITEFLIES

Whiteflies are minute sucking insects of the family Aleyrodidae. Adults have rounded wings covered with snowy, waxy powder. The insects gather on undersides of leaves and generally go unnoticed, unless they're disturbed, in which case they fly out in numbers.

Whiteflies attach their eggs to undersides of leaves, where they hatch in 4 to 12 days. At first, the nymphs (larvae) are pale yellow, six-legged crawlers that move about slowly as they feed by sucking sap from leaves. After the first molt they lose their legs, at which point they resemble soft-bodied scale covered with wax. Whitefly damage can be recognized as *leaves becoming thin in substance and yellow in color and wilt and die or get covered with black mold.*

Generally these aren't especially serious pests, but they can cause damage if left unchecked. Scale and mealybug are very persistent, but whiteflies can be easily eliminated with a few applications of systemics—i.e. pesticides absorbed through the root system and drawn through the sap up into the leaves of the plant.

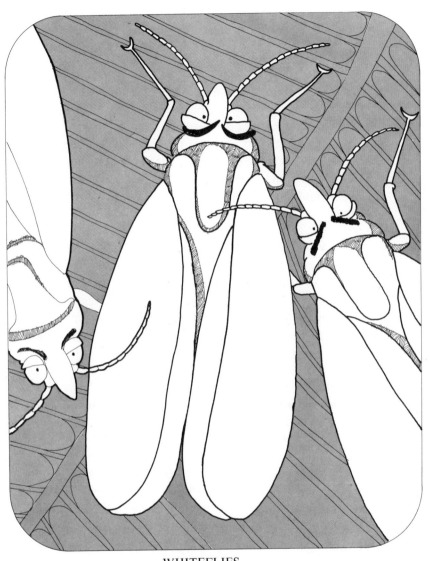

WHITEFLIES

Not-So-Common Insects

This group of insects isn't as often seen as the other group of houseplant insects, but occasionally they do attack indoor plants. Because they are less well known than other insects, some precautions should be taken against them if they attack. Some are quite harmful to plants, others not so much. Included in this category are millipedes, nematodes, slugs and snails, sow bugs, and other crawly things.

MILLIPEDES

Sometimes called thousand-legged worms, these insects belong to the class Diplopoda and are 1 inch long, hard-shelled, cylindrical insects with two pairs of legs on each of their many segments. Millipedes are hardly pretty, although they do come in colors: brown, pink, or gray. These are the insects you'll find coiled up like watch springs under pots or in soil. *Millipedes are dangerous because they feed on plant roots, thus weakening the plant and causing wounds where more serious bacterial disease might start.*

The female lays about 300 eggs in soil or on the surface. The eggs hatch in about 3 weeks and grow slowly; there may be only one generation a year—not much compared to other insects, but enough. Some millipedes are carnivorous-eating insects, but it's hard to tell the good guys from the bad ones, so my advice is get rid of any of them.

Some millipedes are particularly interesting because

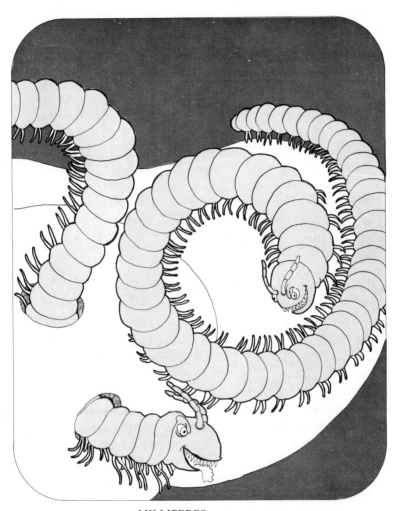

MILLIPEDES

they have an affinity for Philodendrons. This group, technically known as *Orthomorpha gracilis*, is dark brown to black and quite common on houseplants.

SPRINGTAILS

The name is rather cute but the springtail is a harmful insect. *It eats leaves, leaving small round holes,* and while it is not a devastating culprit that can ruin a plant in a short time, it can cause enough damage to warp the psyche of any decent plant. The insects jump and propel themselves around with tail-like appendages. They hide in soil, are very tiny, and have chewing or piercing mouth parts.

The springtail gathers where there is excessive dampness and because they are difficult to see they can accumulate quickly. However, unlike some insects, they are easy to eliminate with proper controls. In general while not a very damaging insect, who wants holey leaves?

LEAF MINERS

These insects feed between leaf surfaces and may be the larvae of flies, beetles, or moths. *Blisters appear on the leaves* as the insect tunnels its merry way. It takes a while to notice the damage and by then the leaf is destroyed, but not the plant. So in essence these are minor enemies (if I am allowed a pun on words). Seriously, these are not often found on house plants, but I have included them because they do on occasion attack some of the gesneriads, which are favorite houseplants. But by and large, they stay outdoors where there is a better selection of fare to dine upon.

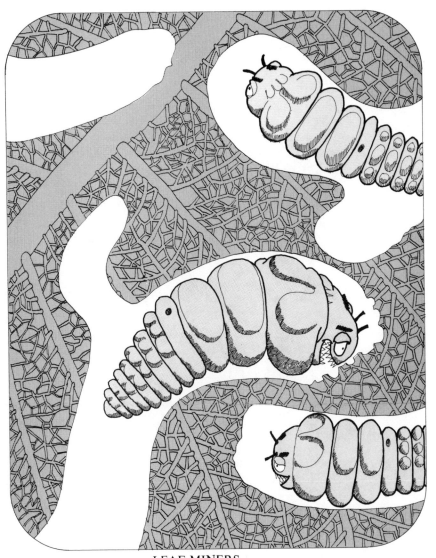

LEAF MINERS

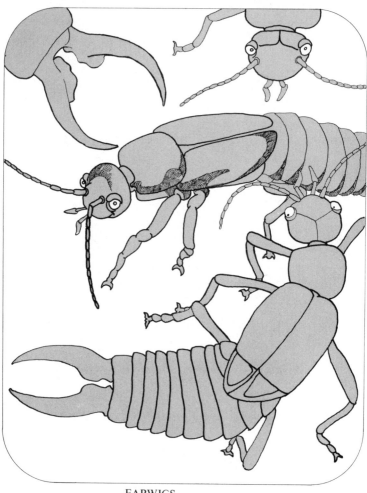

EARWIGS

Earwigs

These are ugly insects with a tail appendage that re-
sembles forceps. They have no right to be in your home

damaging your plants, but do occasionally forsake the outdoors for an indoor vacation. They are nocturnal and will inhabit dark places. And don't be too surprised to find them in closets, or on furniture. They have little gourmet tendencies and seem to dine on most anything at hand including your plants. *Telltale signs of earwigs are damaged leaves.*

NEMATODES

Nematodes are animals, not insects, and their end result is a disease like root knot rather than eaten foliage or other insect symptoms. These eel-like worms are more damaging than you may think. As they feed they can inflict great damage to plants, *causing stunted plants with lack of vigor.* They also *cause wounds in which rot and bacteria can develop and then attack plants.* Other symptoms of nematodes may be yellow or brown wedge-shaped areas on leaves, especially African violets and ferns.

The worms are invisible to the naked eye, so here's a case where you must use the process of elimination to determine the culprit. Most plant nematodes live in and near the roots, although some inhabit stems and leaves. If you suspect a plant has nematode problems, dig up some soil near the crown of the plant (with some roots), place it in a plastic bag, and mail the bag to your County Agricultural Agency for positive identification.

The best prevention against nematodes is a sterile soil. However, if infestation has started, you can use V-C-13 (a nemacide). Because this is poisonous you might opt to discard the plant rather than to risk chemicals in the home.

Sow Bugs

Sow bugs (pill bugs) aren't a serious threat to indoor plants, but occasionally they can be found on a Philodendron or other foliage plant. These are pests, gray to black, oval-shaped and hard-shelled, and infest soils, where they will *occasionally attack plant roots*. Related to crayfish, sow bugs aren't particularly desirable to have around the house. They're excellent scavengers that eat rotting plant parts, but they can become a problem. Look for these miniature armadillos in soil or under pots.

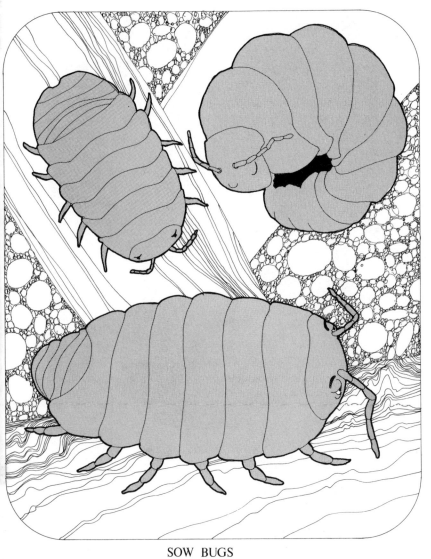

SOW BUGS

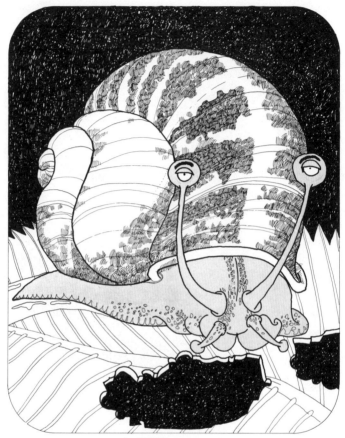

SNAIL

SNAILS AND SLUGS

It seems nobody loves a snail or slug except perhaps another snail or slug. Although they generally stay outdoors, I have, from time to time, found them in my garden room. Snails look like snails (the kind people eat), so there's no sense in describing them. Slugs are much like snails but lack a shell. Both feed at night, and during the

SLUGS

day hide under pots or in other dark out-of-the-way places, not wanting to see you as much as you don't want to see them. *Snails and slugs can damage leaves by chewing the edges (they're prodigious eaters) or by making small holes, and they can, if unchecked, skeletonize foliage.*

QUICK REFERENCE CHART

List of insects and suggested chemical preventives

INSECTS	APPEARANCE	WHAT THEY ATTACK	DAMAGE	CONTROL
Ants	Easily recognized	Many plants	Help establish insect colonies	Many ant baits (check local stores)
Aphids	Oval, red, brown, black insects, 1/8-inch diameter	Begonias, Citrus, Dieffenbachia, Gardenia, Palm, others	Curled leaves; limp growth	Rotenone, Pyrethrum, Black Leaf 40
Earwigs	Brown beetlelike insects	Many plants	Chew leaves or eat holes in them	Malathion
Leaf miners (many kinds)	Larvae of various insects	African violets and other Gesneriads	Blistered leaves; spotted and blotched	Diazinon
Mealybugs	White, cottony	Many plants	Plants wilt; stunted growth	Black Leaf 40; Rotenone Pyrethrum
Millipedes	Multilegged, segmented hard-shelled insects	Philodendron particularly	Chew young growth; feed on roots	Hand pick
Mites (red spider) (not true insects)	Minute, rust-colored	Almost all plants	Discolor leaves	Systemics, Dimite
Nematodes	Microscopic worms	Many plants	Stunted plants; lack of vigor	V-C-13, or discard plant

INSECTS	APPEARANCE	WHAT THEY ATTACK	DAMAGE	CONTROL
Scale	Tiny, hard, and oval insects	Cacti, Camellia, Bromeliads, Palms, Ferns, many other plants	Leaf and stem damage	Diazinon, Black Leaf 40
Snails, Slugs (not insects, but common pests)	Easily recognized	Many plants	Eat foliage	Any snail bait without metaldehyde (Snarol or Cory's Snail Bait are fine)
Sow bugs	Gray to black oval-shaped, hard-shelled insects	Several plants	Eat roots	Change soil
Springtails	Tiny black jumping bugs	Mainly seedlings	Round holes in leaves	Malathion
Thrips	Tiny winged insects, flealike	Ficus plants Asparagus fern, Begonias	Cause leaves to become silvery or curled	Malathion
Whiteflies	Tiny winged or wingless insects	Piggyback plant, Coffee plant, Fuchsias, Lantana, other plants	Leaves turn yellow, mottled or striped	Systemics

For information on types of insecticides and how to use them see Chapter 5.

4 · *Plant Diseases*

I REALIZE that the previous chapter about insects and plants wasn't too enjoyable and now I am throwing plant diseases into the brew. But, it is the purpose of this book to stir your healing powers so when diseases strike you will know what to do. Let us launch into the subject with a light hand but a strong mind.

Plant diseases are as natural in the scheme of things as insects and birds. Disease is an environmental factor that keeps each of the many thousands of living organisms in balance with one another. Quite frankly, most diseases are caused by those culprits—insects. Few general plant books have delved into these maladies. However, all dead plants don't die because of insects; plant diseases take a good toll. A plant disease such as botrytis is not that complicated and can be eliminated. Virus disease (as in human beings) is something else again; it requires some special care if you want to save plants.

Diseases will be minor, but they can become major if allowed to go unchecked.

Ailments that strike plants are manifested in their effects or visible symptoms—spots, blights, rots, mildew, rusts, and so on. Many plant diseases may result in similar external symptoms but may be caused by widely different microorganisms that require completely different methods of control. Positive identification of the disease must be made to ensure positive remedies.

Some plant diseases attack foliage or stems or twigs, flowers, or roots. Diseases in general can be grouped as being caused by either unfavorable growing conditions or by a parasite (bacteria, fungi, viruses). Unfavorable growing conditions—lack of humidity, watering, too much feeding—add to disease hazard too. Now we're concerned with disease caused by bacteria, fungi, and viruses. These are infectious diseases that can be easily spread to other plants.

Bacteria

Bacteria are minute, one-celled plants that lack chlorophyll. Because they can't make their own food, they dine on plants. Bacteria multiply by dividing in half every 20 to 60 minutes, depending upon favorable conditions. They enter plants through naturally occurring minute wounds and small openings. Once inside, they multiply rapidly and start to break down plant tissue (bacteria can move within the plant sap).

Bacteria are spread by human beings when they cultivate or prune already diseased plants or use dirty tools. Animals, soil, insects, water, and dust also carry bacteria that can attack plants.

The most common types of disease caused by bacteria are soft rots, leaf spots, blights, stem rots, and wilts. (There are others too, mentioned later.)

Fungi

Fungi are plants that lack chlorophyll and get their sustenance from living plants or nonliving organic matter. Some fungi start life as spores and divide into fungus bodies. These penetrate a plant by growing into a wound, through a natural opening, or by forcing their entrance directly through the plant's stems or leaves. Spores are carried by wind, water, insects, people, and equipment. Spores can, if necessary, remain dormant for many years; when they persist in the soil they are especially difficult to kill.

(Some fungi don't produce spores. They multiply by forming masses of *hyphae* or form a fungus body that divides into fragments which are broken off and carried by water, wind, and other agents.) Like bacteria, fungi are more likely to multiply in shady and damp conditions rather than in hot and dry situations. Generally moisture is essential in their reproduction, and they must penetrate plant parts (and thus infect plant parts) so they have a place to live. Fungi cause rusts, smuts, mildews, some leaf spot, and blights.

Viruses

Viruses are as complex in plants as they are in humans. Viruses are protein molecules that multiply, mutate, and infect and act as living organisms in a plant. They're smaller than fungi and can't be seen with an ordinary microscope. The most common types of viruses that cause plant diseases are mosaic, spotted wilt, ring spot, and stunt. The symptoms of viruses are highly variable, even on different varieties of the same plant; viruses are spread by insects or from diseased to healthy plants by contact. There are ways to eliminate bacterial and fungal infections in plants, but absolute cures of virus infections are still beyond our reach.

Nematodes

As discussed in the insect section, these worms' end result is plant disease. To grow and reproduce, the nematodes usually need plant juices; thus they reduce the vigor of the plant and make it more susceptible to fungus and bacterial diseases. (See Chapter 3.)

Specific Diseases

BOTRYTIS

Botrytis can be brought on by cool, damp periods. Symptoms are soft tan to brown colored spots or blotches on leaves, stems, or flowers. The parts attacked may also be covered with tannish–gray mold. The fungus enters through wounds or dying leaves.

Control: Discard and burn infected parts. Give plants more space and shade. Avoid high humidities, and provide good air circulation. Spray with Zineb or Captan.

Plants attacked: African violets, Amaryllis, Amazon lily, Begonias, Cacti, Caladiums, Cyclamen, Gardenia, Geranium, Tradescantia

MOSAIC

This virus disease has variable symptoms. Generally leaves have a mild or severe yellowing or light and dark green areas forming a mosaic or mottled effect. Sometimes white or yellow ring or line patterns occur. Leaves will be distorted or cupped.

Control: Control insects, especially aphids.
Plants attacked: Many

FUNGUS RING SPOT

Look for a spot(s) on foliage, often marked with concentric zones. When disease progresses, spots become enlarged, forming blotches. Leaves may wither and die prematurely. Fungus ring spot, the most common plant disease, is caused by too much moisture and wetness, high humidity, and water splashed on foliage.

Control: Remove leaves with spots and discard. Use Captan, Zineb fungicide, or Benomyl.
Plants attacked: Geranium, African violet, Cacti, Dracaena, Tolmiea
NOTE: Certain leaf spots have special names such as anthracnose.

RING SPOT DISEASE

LEAF SPOT DISEASE

Bacterial Leaf Spot

Water-soaked spots or streaks on leaves or stems that later turn gray, brown, or black can be an indication of bacterial leaf spot. Another clue is foliage that withers and dies.

Control: Same as for fungus ring spot.
Plants attacked: Geraniums, African violets, Gloxinia
and other Gesneriads, Cacti, Dracaena

BACTERIAL WILT (brown rot; blight)

The symptoms of these diseases vary, but generally
plants show dark green and water-soaked areas on
leaves. These expand rapidly, and then leaves dry and
turn brown. Occasionally a shiny crust appears on affected leaves. Leaves may wilt or turn yellow, and stems
often shrivel and dry out.

Control: Collect and burn affected parts.
Plants attacked: Many

POWDERY MILDEW

Indications of this disease are a white–to–light-grayish
powdery coating on leaves, buds, or young shoots. Dwarf-
ing may occur, and leaves may yellow and wither. Mildew
spots may enlarge to cover entire leaf. The disease is most
likely to start from cool nights followed by warm days or
poor air circulation.

Control: Avoid overcrowding and damp conditions. In-
    crease air circulation and night temperature. Dust
    or spray with Karathane every 10 days if plant is
    severely attacked.
Plants attacked: Acalypha, African violets, Pilea, Ivy,
    piggyback plant, siderasis

POWDERY MILDEW ON LEAVES

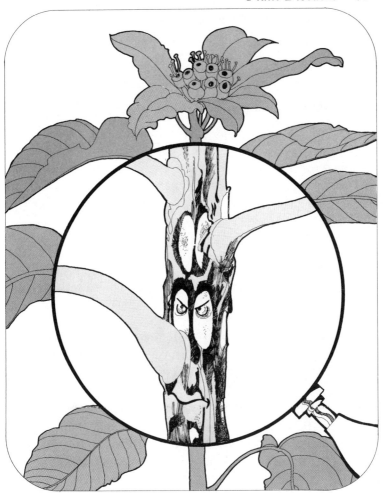

SCAB

Symptoms of scab are variable but generally appear as raised or sunken areas on leaves or stems.

Control: Raise temperature and reduce air humidity.

Keep water off leaves.

Plants attacked: Abutilon, Orchids, Dracaena, Dieffenbachia, Crassula, Echeveria

Sooty Mold

Sooty mold appears as dark brown or black splotches
on leaves or stems. The fungus occurs on honeydew
patches formed by insects such as aphids and scale. Not
a serious disease, but it can disfigure a plant.

Control: Keep insects from plants.
Plants attacked: Ivy, Citrus trees, Oleander, Palms,
Philodendron

Verticillium Wilt

Leaves start to yellow and fall, generally from the bottom of plant, progressing upward. Wilting is common.
Disease enters plant through wounds.

Control: Discard infected parts. Keep plants free of in-
sects.
Plants attacked: Abutilon, Avocado, Begonia, Geranium,
Pittosporum, Crown-of-thorns

STEM ROT INFECTION

CROWN AND STEM ROT DISEASE

This little plague has befallen your plants when you see mushy and soft stems and crowns. Worse yet, if you haven't been paying attention, the crowns will become simply a rotten water-soaked mess. The plant goes into a state of shock (you would too if your ear, say, started to rot) and within a short time the plant collapses.

Control: Cut away infected parts and discard; dust with
       Captan or Zineb. If entire plant is affected, dis-
       card all.
Plants attacked: Many

ROOT ROT

These are fungi that get right to the root of the plant and in fast time too. You will see the invasion (not really) by leaves that wilt and new growth that just doesn't grow but instead dies back. At first glance when you see the wilted leaves you may rush for the watering can. Don't! It will just make things worse.

Control: Repot plant in fresh soil; wash roots with luke-
       warm tap water. Or douse soil with a fungicide
       such as Captan.
Plants attacked: Mainly Gesneriads and Succulents

See Chapter 5 for more information on fungicides.

ROOT ROT DISEASE

DAMPING-OFF DISEASE

This is a soil-borne fungus that mainly attacks seedlings. The stem is the first to collapse and then the leaves go. Overnight the seedlings may die. The prime cause of damping-off is unsterilized soils (high humidity does the rest).

Control: Quite simply, always use sterilized soil for sowing seed and avoid keeping the small plants in overbearing moist conditions.

5 · *Is There a Doctor in the House?*

IF YOUR PLANTS ARE ATTACKED by insects or disease, you'll have to know something about remedies to make them well. You don't have to become a specialist, but some basic facts about pesticides and fungicides are necessary.

In the home, where plants are confined to pots of soil, we have many less problems to cope with (thankfully) than with outdoor plants. Some of the safer chemicals such as rotenone and pyrethrum (derived from plants) are natural remedies, and chemicals such as *malathion* and *diazinon,* although poisonous, can, if absolutely necessary, be used indoors. The main precaution is that all insecticides (natural or man-made) be handled carefully and put out of reach of children and pets. I keep my plant medicine kit on high shelves.

There are also a host of good, old-fashioned remedies for eliminating insects from plants. I use these frequently because they're safe, easy to use, and don't smell bad (if you've ever used Malathion at home, you know that the unpleasant odor lingers for some time).

Insecticides

Because there are so many insecticides, fungicides, and what not and so many trade names for these products, it's essential that you read this chapter. Using the wrong remedy can actually be lethal to your plant. There are poisons for specific insects. There are combination poisons that combat several pests at once. Contact poisons that are sprayed on the insects coat the leaves with pesticide and this can injure plants like Ferns, Palms and Orchids. Other chemicals work as stomach poisons, applied to foliage to kill insects when they suck or chew leaves. Some insecticides are broad spectrum and kill many bugs (Malathion for example) while others are specific for, say, mites, such as Dimite.

Some chemicals come in a granular form, sprinkled on soil before watering; others are soluble, to be mixed with water. In this case, use a spray bottle. These sprayers do not need hose attachments so they can be used indoors. There are also powders or dusts for plants which also require special equipment. There are also systemic insecticides and fungicides (explained later).

With all chemicals, repeated applications are necessary to get all insects and their succeeding brood. Spray the entire plant, including and especially the undersides of leaves.

There are also soil fumigants but don't be tempted to use these. They are not necessary for indoor gardening.

Small pressurized spray cans (aerosols) of general-purpose insecticides are also available, and to further complicate matters there are combinations of insecticides and fertilizers. (These feed and kill at the same time.)

Because there are so many killers, it's wise to know something more about them:

1. *Chlorinated hydrocarbons.* This group includes the deadliest poisons such as aldrin, dieldrin, heptachlor, and lindane. I mention the specific names so you will know and avoid them. These chemicals are simply not needed for indoor plants.

2. *Organic phosphates.* This group includes a large array of chemical killers, some safer than others. They're basically nerve poisons. The best are malathion and diazinon, which control many destructive insects and are fairly but not completely safe for use. Malathion smells terrible and must be mixed and *sprayed.* Diazinon and spectracide are toxic, but knock out scale, mites, wireworms, and other insects.

3. *Carbamates.* These include fungicides and herbicides. They are generally broad spectrum chemicals; that is, they kill many types of insects. Sevin, well known, is widely used for combating mealybugs, mites, and cutworms.

4. *Miticides.* These are chemicals specifically for controlling mites. Dimite is good and is less toxic than say Tedion or Ovotran. Kelthane is highly toxic but is frequently used.

5. *Aerosols.* Read labels carefully on cans; some contain pyrethrins, which are highly poisonous and not needed for home control of pests on plants. (Usually sold as Indoor Plant Spray.) Aerosols are convenient (no mixing)

but expensive, and as indicated, quite poisonous. (Aerosol cans themselves are now under scrutiny by government agencies as to their harmful effect on the atmosphere. Watch newspapers for current information.) Avoid outdoor aerosol insect sprays; these are much too strong to use on indoor plants.

6. *Systemics*. Available under several trade names such as Isotox, Meta-Systox. These chemicals control many but not all insects. Systemics are applied to the soil and absorbed by the roots of the plant through the sap; the sap then becomes poisonous to insects. While systemics offer good insect protection, they are highly toxic.

7. *Botanical Insecticides*. These are by far the safest preparations. Rotenone, pyrethrum and ryania are plant extracts or ground powders of plants. Sold under various trade names, they control many insects and should be your first line of defense against houseplant pests. Black Leaf 40 may also be classified as a botanical because it is derived from tobacco. This has been on the market for many, many years and widely used. Black Leaf 40 kills a wide variety of insects and effectively, but it is more poisonous than rotenone or pyrethrum.

8. *Poison Baits*. These control snails and slugs; most contain metaldehyde, which is highly poisonous. Look for Snarol or Cory's Snail Bait, which don't have metaldehyde, and are relatively safe to use indoors. Ant-bait and ant-cups are also available under different trade names.

9. *Nematocides*. These are contact or fumigant poisons used for the soil to eliminate nematodes. V-C Nemacide is quite toxic, V-C-13, a safer alternative. Some plants such as palms and ferns are very sensitive to nematocides so be forewarned.

Pyrethrum is a daisylike flower; when dried and powdered it is an effective insect killer. (Photo by USDA)

How to Use Chemicals

No matter what poison you use (if you use any), follow directions on the package to the letter. However, first I would suggest using botanicals. If these don't work, then try Malathion. If that doesn't work and stronger chemicals are needed, the decision is yours. When using chemicals indoors, always follow these basic rules:

1. Isolate the infested plant while it is being treated and keep it away from pets and children.

2. Keep all chemicals and equipment together, and store them in a closed carton, out of reach. Certainly avoid keeping them in the kitchen or bathroom.

3. Never use a chemical on a plant that has bone-dry soil.

4. Never spray or dust plants in direct sunlight.

5. Always use a spray at proper spraying distance.

6. Try to douse the insects if they're in sight.

7. Don't use contact chemicals on Orchids; there are other ways to combat insects on these plants. See Chapter 6.

8. Take the plants outside for treatment if at all possible. If this isn't possible, keep windows in your apartment open because ventilation is vital, not to the plant, but to you.

9. Don't bother with ladybugs, praying mantises, or any other beneficial insects for indoor plants' protection, because they won't stay; their union demands outdoor conditions. These insects really must have a prodigious

supply of other insects to exist—far more than your plants, no matter how infected, can supply.

Fungicides

These are contact poisons that kill or inhibit growth of fungi and bacteria. They come in dust form, or in powders and emulsions that are combined with a solvent so they can mix with water in a liquid spray when diluted. There are also systemic fungicides such as Benomyl. There are many fungicides; those listed below are just a few of them.

1. *Captan.* An organic fungicide. Effective and safe for molds and rots. Widely used.

2. *Ferbam.* A very effective fungicide for rusts or anthracnose.

3. *Karathane.* Highly effective remedy for powdery mildew. Do not use in hot (over 80° F) temperatures.

4. *Sulfur.* This is an old and inexpensive fungicide and still good for many diseases, including leaf spot, mildew, and scab. Liquid and dry sulfur also available. Do not use in very hot weather.

5. *Zineb.* Used for botrytis, stem and crown rot disease; one of the best remedies.

6. *Benomyl.* A systemic used for many bacterial and fungus diseases.

7. *Bordeaux Mixture.* An old remedy to control certain fungus leaf spot diseases but being replaced by newer fungicides.

8. *Agrimycin.* An antibiotic for many kinds of bacterial diseases.

Old-fashioned Remedies

If you're against poisons in the home, as I am, try the following safe and effective do-it-yourself methods of fighting bugs:

1. Handpicking. This is time-consuming, and unless you use a toothpick, it's impossible to pick up tiny and elusive scale or aphids. However, patience is a virtue and this is one way to learn it.

2. Soap and water. For many insects, such as aphids and mealybugs, a solution of ½ pound of laundry bar soap (not detergent) to one gallon of water will work. Spray or douse the plant with this mixture, and repeat applications about every 3 days for a 9-day period.

3. Alcohol. Alcohol on cotton swabs will effectively remove mealybugs and sometimes aphids.

4. Tobacco. Use a solution of old tobacco steeped in water for several days to get rid of scale. Douse it on the insects. Repeat several times. Eventually you'll win.

5. Water spray. If you have the patience and time, spray plants and insects daily with a strong water spray. Eventually the bugs give up because even they don't like to be hit with water.

6. Wipe leaves frequently. This simple step eliminates eggs before they hatch and saves a lot of trouble.

Cotton swabs with alcohol will eliminate mealybugs when you don't want to use chemicals in the home. (Photo by USDA)

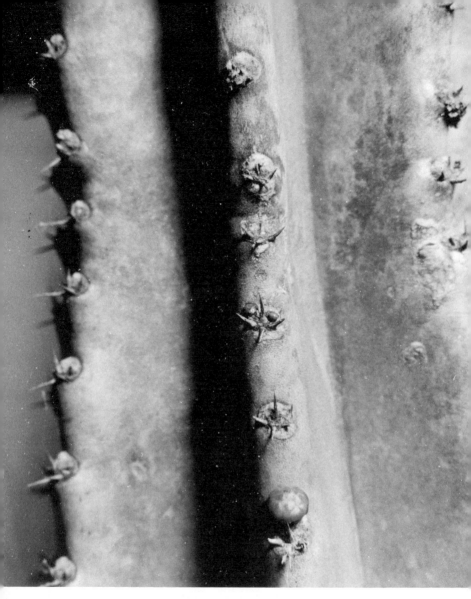

On the middle rib of this cactus you can see scale insects; these can be picked off with toothpicks or eliminated with a solution of old tobacco and soapy water. (Photo by Matthew Barr)

7. Food. Use stale beer in small bottle caps near pots to catch snails and slugs. Potatoes cut in half supposedly will lure snails and slugs away, but with the price of potatoes—well! Salt, however, is still cheap, and when poured on slugs it makes them intolerably ill (you too when you see it).

8. Hot water. Hot water (90° F) poured over the top of the soil of a plant *chases* springtails into a saucer, where you can wash them away.

9. I know of no home remedy for root nematode. If they attack, discard the plant rather than run the risk of infecting other plants.

6 · *Preventative Medicine*

THESE AREN'T REALLY MEDICATIONS but ways and means
of keeping pests and diseases from striking your plants
or spreading. As mentioned, observation is the key to
catching trouble before it starts, but there are other
rather simple but important ways to thwart a minor (or
major) plague in your indoor garden. Some of these
methods, which may seem unorthodox, are based on my
own experiments on houseplants—the ones that worked
as well as the ones that didn't; that is, I unwittingly
murdered a plant. Other methods are just pure common
sense; perhaps you've heard them before, but they're
worth mentioning again.

If a disease or an insect is introduced into your garden
area, it generally comes from a new arrival, a recently
purchased plant. So it makes good sense to inspect before
you buy. Sometimes this isn't possible in the rush of buying plants, but at least scan the plant as it is from head
to toe; a complete examination can be made later at home.
Sick plants and even suspected victims should be isolated
from your indoor plants.

New Arrivals

At the store, closely observe and inspect every leaf and stem of a plant. It looks healthy, so you buy it. Yet when you get it home it still may have bugs. Where are they? In the soil! These unwanted guests can be quickly brought out of hiding by soaking the pot to its rim in a sink of water for about 2 hours. Any little visitors hiding will be flushed to the surface.

Another simple method of making sure you know your plants are insect-free is to hose down leaves and stems repeatedly before you introduce them into the collection. And still another way, and this is important, is to hold the plant over a piece of newspaper and shake it—not too hard, but hard enough to dislodge any clinging critters. Often insects hide under leaf axils or stems and are really difficult to see with the naked eye. An orchid I received in a shipment looked rather clean to me when I opened the package. But by accident I knocked over the pot. From one of the leaves crawled the loveliest black beetle I've seen in years. It was large enough for me to see on the plant, but it had camouflaged itself so perfectly I missed it.

While you are making your examination of the plant, also inspect the pot. Many times old crusted clay pots harbor insect eggs or the insects themselves, on either the top or bottom. Give the pot a good scrubbing with hot tap water.

If there are some leaf spots or brown edges on leaves, be ruthless and trim them away. These may be natural tendencies and nothing to worry about, but since marred leaves add nothing to the beauty of the plant, why not remove them? These spots could be the start of fungus disease, so better be safe than sorry. After cutting any stem or leaf (with a sterile knife run over a match flame), seal the wounds with powdered charcoal. This procedure prevents possible viral infection.

Here's an important step that can save many new plants from becoming sick. When you get a new plant, remember that it has been grown under ideal conditions in a greenhouse. The move to new surroundings is apt to be somewhat of a shock to the plant. For this reason it's a good idea to acclimatize the plant gradually; that is, don't immediately put it in a hot sunny place. It was grown in

Direct sun and too much heat killed this Zygocactus and it is too late to save the plant.

Underwatering was the culprit here and this Platycerium (staghorn fern) needs immediate care. Even then, it may not survive.

a bright, very humid greenhouse—moist, but not overly warm. Put your new plant in a shady, somewhat cool place, and water moderately for a few days. Then move it to brighter light with warmer temperatures and more water and then finally to its permanent place—in sun or whatever. If this sounds like a lot of work, it is, but it will prevent a plant from becoming weakened; weakened plants are more prone to attack than healthy ones.

This Fern suffers from underwatering; fronds have shriveled and are beyond saving. Cut away and trim plant.

Instruments and Care

For cutting and trimming plant parts I use a pocket-knife and a small manicure scissors. That's about all you'll need. I subject both these instruments to match flames before and after I do any cutting. This procedure leaves a black residue on the knife or scissors, and if you use the instrument while still heated, the plant tissue will be seared and thus close the wound itself without charcoal applications.

A most important rule is not to splash water from plant to plant. Fungus and other diseases can be waterborne, so be neat. Also, it's a good idea to wash your hands after handling one plant and before you handle another to prevent carrying a disease from an affected plant to another.

When repotting plants, use your hands rather than old potting sticks or whatever. Any kind of tool can harbor insect eggs or diseases, so why not be careful? Besides, you can do a much better job potting with your fingers than with tools.

Observation

If a plant looks wilted, has yellow leaves, or generally isn't growing well in spite of good culture, and you suspect something amiss, remove it from the indoor garden and isolate it in, say, an unheated pantry or garage where it will have cool temperatures, and give it less water. Observe for a few days whether this is doing any good. If the plant still fails, unpot it and inspect the soil for problems, such as springtail or soil mealybug. Examine the roots to see if perhaps root nematodes have left telltale galls. The root system should appear thick and healthy; if not, you may have overwatered the plant or placed it in too large a pot to begin with, and it is possible that "potting down" to a smaller-sized container may stimulate new growth.

Always watch new foliage growth closely, because this is where insects are most likely to attack. The new growth is fresh and green and makes a succulent meal. Many times insect attack starts here, and if you catch it, all you have to do is snip off the fresh leaves. New growth will start, and you've avoided having to get out remedies.

While you're observing, wipe leaves with a damp cloth; this goes a long way in preventing eggs from hatching, eliminating insects you may not see, and preventing insects from starting damage. Don't under any circumstance, use leaf-shining preparations on your plant leaves even if you want to impress guests. It might impress them all right, but it will depress the plants by clogging leaf pores, and plants do breathe through their leaves.

Terminal Cases

Sometimes you may be too late to treat a sick plant. As a result, a stricken plant, loaded with insects or overcome by a virus or disease, is just too far gone to do anything. *Discard* the plant. This is far better than having other

This terminal case of crown rot was caused by overwatering and the plant must be discarded.

plants in the collection stricken. If you can find a healthy, uninfested part of the sick plant—a leaf section or a crown or small stem section—you might try to start a new plant by propagation. Put the plant part in vermiculite in any container with drain holes, and place a plastic bag over it. When it roots—several days to weeks—remove the bag and plant the part in rich soil. With any luck, in a few weeks you'll have an offspring of the plant you reluctantly threw out.

Repairing Damage

No matter how careful you are with plants, accidents do happen: a plant falls, stems are broken, or the crown of the plant is cracked. No need to panic. I've repaired more than one broken stem, and, surprisingly, it works. If the bent stem is still intact, I use a small sliver of wood placed lengthwise to the break, to make a splint, tying it on with string. Often healing occurs, and within a few weeks the half-broken stem is growing again. If the stem is completely broken, cut the fragment away and brush the broken end of the whole plant with charcoal dust. Then try rooting the fragment. If too small, however, throw it away.

If a plant falls and leaves are cracked, remove them, because open wounds are invitation for fungus and bacteria. Even if you hate to do it, throw away the entire leaf or leaves. If the crown of the plant is cracked in pieces, take the largest pieces and pot them. Throw away smaller ones; they won't take.

While not damaged, certain plants such as Dieffenbachias or *Dracaena massangeana*, lose all lower leaves. You're left with a topknot that's more funny to look at than handsome. Can you get new growth to start at the bottom from the main stem or an auxiliary crown? Yes, but not always. So this is where you must make an educated guess. If you're stalwart, cut off some of the side branches, and hope the plant regains vigor and breaks new growth near the bottom. Again, sometimes it does, other times it doesn't. It seems to work well with vining Philodendron, but not with rubber trees or fiddleaf figs.

If a plant is so damaged by insects that all you have left is a scrawny specimen, start pruning. If it's a woody-stemmed plant, cut it back to about 3 inches. Give it good care and humidity; generally, in a few weeks new growth will start and the plant will have been saved. A gold star for the doctor!

Sometimes when a plant is badly damaged by insects, it is wise to cut it down completely. This was done on this Pseudopanax, and within 2 weeks new sprouts started.

7 · Special Cases

YEARS AGO we had pot plants at the window and that was about it. Today we have plants in hanging containers, on shelves under artificial lights, in terrariums, and on display as huge, floor-standing specimens. I think all these facets of gardening deserve some attention because they each have different potential problems. Miniature plants (in terrariums) have certain idiosyncrasies and are grown under different conditions from plants at a window. Treelike plants (very expensive) are mature specimens that need special attention (particularly since they are such a large investment!), and plants in baskets in the air are in their own heavenly world.

Basket Plants

These include the trailing beauties like Plectranthus and kangaroo vine, Chlorophytum (spider plant), and

Cissus discolor is a lovely foliage plant but this one should have had better care. It needs trimming of stems and removal of a few leaves so air can better circulate around the plant.

Tolmiea menziesii (*the piggyback plant*) *is a good basket subject but has lush growth. In such a situation when leaves are crowded, excess water on foliage can lead to bacterial diseases. It is best to trim away a few leaves so air gets to all parts of the plant.*

many other fine plants. The beauty of basket growing is that it creates a lush halo of green at eye level. But when growing plants this way there are certain innate hazards. Be sure to hang plants in such a way that it is convenient to observe and water them regularly. Lazy gardeners will inevitably tend to neglect their hanging gardens as time passes. Lushly grown plants with lots of leaves crammed against each other cut down the light and air that reaches the leaves. Most plants insist on good ventilation, and overcrowded conditions can cause mildew if there is too much moisture sprayed on the plant. Overcrowding can also lead to a real infestation of insects because they can travel far in little time.

So occasionally, if you are growing basket beauties, trim a few leaves here and there. Rather than giving the plant a sparse look, it should improve the appearance. If you're against cutting leaves away (which sometimes can ruin an effect you're trying to create), then hose down the plant early in the morning, make sure there is good ventilation so it dries by night, and keep observing your big beautiful halos of green.

Terrariums

These lovely cases—glass or plastic—have become immensely popular and rightly so. There's no easier way to grow plants than in terrariums, where they are "self-watering"—furnishing their own moisture (through transpiration) that then accumulates on the sides of the case and rolls down into the soil. But again, there are some inherent hazards. A terrarium can get very humid, in fact too humid, leading to fungus disease of one sort or another.

It's better to trim plants somewhat and give them growing space than to let the miniature greenery become a jungle. Like a natural jungle, there's then more room for insects and disease, so if the terrarium gets too much inside moisture—and you'll see this as heavy condensation on the glass—remove the lid, stopper, or top for a few hours to let the case dry out somewhat. Never spray insecticides into a terrarium because in most cases tiny plants in small areas can't take strong chemicals and are liable to expire, not just one plant but all of them. It's bet-

Closed terrariums such as this need close observation; if condensation forms on glass, remove lid or top so air can get to plants. Otherwise, insects and diseases can result.

ter to remove the victim and replace it than to subject all plants to the chemical barrage.

Occasionally in terrariums you'll notice salts (white residues) developing at the soil line. This is an indication that soon something may go awry. The salts may be toxic and eventually might sour the soil and thus harm plants. What to do? Replant. Make a new arrangement and be safe rather than sorry.

This terrarium is much too crowded; some trimming should be done so each plant has space to grow. Otherwise, crowding coupled with excessive moisture can mean trouble.

Decorator Plants

These are the big giants that cost so much money but are so lovely in the home. Fortunately for your pocketbook and the plant, mature specimens are rarely bothered by insects or disease. They're at the peak of their health, robust, and a healthy plant is a tough one that rarely be-

This lovely Philodendron decorator plant is in fine health. It is meticulously trained to the tree bark stake.

comes sick. Still, nothing is perfect, and things can go amiss. It's impossible to soak big plants in the sink, but washing leaves with a damp cloth isn't, so do it. Spray them regularly with water. Remember that those biggies are a real investment, and you want them with you a long time.

If a large plant is infested with pests, this is a case where some medication is in order. If possible, move the plant outdoors, and use the appropriate spray for the specific pests (red spider, mealybug, and so forth) as outlined in Chapter 3.

If your favorite big plant starts to die for no apparent reason—no insects on it, no signs of disease—sit back and think things out. What have you done or changed that might be causing the trouble? For example, I had a lovely 7-foot bamboo palm that thrived for about 2 years in a living room corner. When redecorating, I decided to move it to another location. I did, and the plant developed a beautiful case of mealybug in about 2 months. Why? It was drier in this spot perhaps, or air currents were wrong. Once you have a big plant in a place where it's growing, try to leave it there. It has adjusted to the light and humidity of that area, and moving can weaken it (your back too).

Plants Under Artificial Light

Growing plants under artficial light has attracted legions of followers in the last few years and rightly so. It is a good way to grow plants where there is little natural light. Under controlled conditions where there is constant light, plants grow all the time, perhaps better than they would at windows, where on gray days plants rest, and in winter grow less.

Generally, the light garden is crowded with plants so there is more chance for insects and disease. Giving plants ample space to grow and providing ventilation is very important in keeping insects down and fungus from starting in any situation. So in your light-units, see that leaves of plants are not touching other plants; be sure there is adequate movement of air to prevent any problems.

Because plants grow all the time under lights, the winter dormancy that occurs with plants at windows is skipped. This means constant observation on your part to be sure insects haven't started to work. And finally, with plants under lights, once insects start they travel from one plant to another quickly. And disease too can wipe out a collection in a short time. So in essence, be alert, and work at your gardening. You will have to keep plants in good shape when growing them under lights.

Gift Plants

These are special cases because the plants always seem to die about a month after people get them. Most are condemned as indoor plants when given to you, including Cinerarias, Azaleas, Cyclamen, and Hydrangeas. Grown under ideal greenhouse conditions, these will last in the average home for only a few months, and that's the way it is. The grower knows it, the florist who sells it knows it, so you might as well know it. However, there are some gift plants that can be saved; these include the Christ-

Observe decorator plants like this fiddleleaf fig (Ficus lyrata) *frequently to be sure insects haven't invaded. It is quite easy even in a photo to inspect vulnerable places such as leaf axils and stems.*

mas cactus (*Zygacactus truncatus*), Poinsettias, pepper plant, Gardenia, Fuchsia, and Gloxinia.

When you first get a gift plant, keep it in a cool and bright but not sunny place. High temperatures and hot sun will kill it quickly. When the plant finishes blooming, let it rest a little again in coolness, and in a few months cut it back. If possible, summer it outdoors in fresh soil in a new container. Take it in when cool weather starts, or in a few months, and continue to grow it, but this time give it plenty of light, humidity, and warmth. Try it! It sometimes works.

I Like You . . . Don't You Like Me?

At cocktail parties, have you met people that for some reason you simply couldn't talk to for more than two minutes? Or people you immediately took a dislike to? Well, this can and does happen with plants and people too. This phenomenon (call it what you will) has happened to me on three occasions in some fifteen years of growing plants. One plant was a lovely large Fern that I took care of with meticulous culture. All conditions were right, but the plant simply refused to grow. I moved it around. I waited several weeks to see if it would acclimatize to the apartment conditions. But nothing worked. It simply wouldn't adjust to me, I guess. I gave the plant to a friend, and within a month it was blushing with new growth and as beautiful as a picture postcard. Coincidence? Maybe. The point is: If you have a specific plant that apparently doesn't do well, and you're giving it the best of care and it still doesn't do well for months, get rid of it. It simply may not like you. Give it to a friend, and maybe you'll have played cupid. The other two plants I had that found me intolerable (or vice versa) were a gigantic fiddleleaf fig (it dropped leaves whenever I looked at it), and a *Monstera deliciosa* (swisscheese plant) which sulked for ten months. In each case, the plants were given to friends and they survived. The plants, that is.

8 · Popular Plants and Their Characteristics

IT CANNOT BE REPEATED TOO OFTEN that proper care and cultural conditions—water, light, humidity, soil—are vastly important in keeping plants free of insects and diseases. However, just as some people get more colds than others, some plants get more ailments than others. You should know beforehand what to expect from the plants you grow. To simplify the choice of possible plants, I've limited the selection to easily recognizable plant categories such as: Ferns, Palms, Cacti, and Orchids. These plants are generally known to the public, so if you have a Fern, you can turn to this section to see just how much trouble you can anticipate when you select a particular plant (or perhaps it may be trouble-free).

Australian Umbrella Tree (*Schefflera actinophylla*)

This is probably one of the most popular indoor tree-type plants that grows easily and with little care if only given bright light and an evenly moist soil. Generally, the umbrella tree—mature ones especially—are insect-free and rarely troubled by pests or disease. Occasionally, however, younger plants seem to have their share of red spider mites when grown in very dry atmospheres. Mist regularly and always keep leaves clean by washing with a damp cloth.

Begonias

Although subject to their share of ailments, Begonias are such a large group (relatively speaking) that they're almost trouble-free plants. There are several groups: angel-winged, rhizomatous, hirsute, and Rex, to mention only a few. The angel wings are by far the least likely to be bothered by insects, other than aphids or thrips, and these attack infrequently.

The lush rhizomatous and fine hirsutes that do so well indoors occasionally may get mealybugs, powdery mildew, or gray mold blight. Yet because they are such good fast-growing plants for the home, I still recommend them highly.

Rex begonias, those exquisite tapestry-leaved plants, are trouble. Unless exacting conditions are met—humidity, watering, resting—they drop leaves and are subject to various fungus disorders. Wait until you're a "pro" before you tackle these.

In general, Begonias should be watered less frequently than other plants. Avoid misting.

Bromeliads

I've grown hundreds of these and never lost a plant from insect attack or disease. Indeed, these are incredible houseplants and rarely bothered by problems. Insects seem to avoid them, and disease is rare unless you bury the crown in soil and keep it overwatered; then basal rot can occur. Occasionally leaves may become brown at edges, but this is generally from bruising or being brushed by furniture or such rather than disease.

As Bromeliads are natural, tough-leaved plants, you will have little or no problem growing them. The thick leathery leaves of most Bromeliads are just too tough for the average insect.

Cacti and Succulents

Here are two large groups of exciting plants that are so varied and large I can only touch on a few of them. Cacti and succulents store water in their stems and tolerate drought for months. Outdoors they grow in sandy soils, but generally at home, pot them in a balanced soil mix (one with all nutrients) and water regularly. If you don't, the plant won't grow and may develop scab. On the other hand, too much water will cause basal rot. Snails occasionally attack cacti and succulents (mealybugs too, but not so much).

CRASSULA

The favorite species is the jade tree (*Crassula argentea*), and a better plant is tough to find. Almost impossible for insects to bother, but trunks are brittle, so handle carefully.

ECHEVERIAS

These are becoming quite popular. They're prone to mealybugs.

AGAVES

These are big rosette plants that make fine decorator plants. Most are impervious to attack by insects because of their thick heavy leaves and will contract disease only if they're overwatered.

CACTUS

Most of the common cactus you see for sale (in small pots) at stores are seldom bothered with insects or disease.

ZYGOCACTUS, RHIPSALIDOPSIS, SCHLUMBERGERA

Known as Christmas cactus or Easter cactus, depending upon whom you talk to. These are cacti, but require different treatment; they're jungle epiphytes as different from their cactus desert cousins as night from day. They need a potting soil of equal parts fir bark and soil, as well as moisture and shade. Generally trouble-free, although occasionally virus hits a plant.

Dieffenbachias

These are the large-leaved beauties with variegated leaves and stout trunks; they make favorite decorator plants. Although they're beautiful, they're not so easily grown as some plants, and lower leaves have a tendency to turn brown and drop off. Some recent plants I've noticed seem to be victims of *rot:* bottom leaves yellow, turn brown, and drop, and disease escalates, traveling up the plant. An antibiotic is the supposed cure, but the plants I tried it on were either too far gone or the medication just didn't work. Watch when purchasing Dieffenbachias. If you see any yellow leaves or any suspicious foliage at the bottom of the plant, avoid buying it.

Dracaenas

These are members of the lily family and make handsome foliage plants for indoor beauty. Usually, most Dracaenas are rarely bothered by insects or disease. Occasionally, a few mealybugs might gather on undersides of leaves but these are easily eliminated—just pick them off. Most of the species have a single trunk, so there is no worry about too much water at the crown of the plant. These plants are as close to pest free as a houseplant can be.

False Aralia (Dizygotheca)

A popular decorator plant, and lovely, with delicate fronds and wiry stems, but impossible to grow indoors unless you're Luther Burbank. My plants are always attacked by mealybugs or thrips, even under the best of care, and I've had numerous questions about insects and this plant. Avoid if you can resist, or be prepared to administer first aid frequently. To add to their temperamental growing habits, they chill easily and suddenly leaves fall overight. (No one wants a plant that catches cold that quickly.)

Ferns

This group of lovely plants draws more questions about them than any other family. Their afflictions range from brown fronds to insect infestation and sometimes a total collapse of the plant. Because a Fern isn't just a Fern (there are hundreds of species), this information is general; for specific plants you'll have to temper the suggestions. One suggestion for ailing tiny Ferns that seems to work is to move them to a terrarium.

BOSTON FERN (*Nephrolepis exaltata Bostoniensis*)

One of the good indoor Ferns that can take some abuse and rarely is attacked by ailments. However, if fronds touch glass or other obstacles, they'll turn brown at edges. With mature Ferns, remnants of dead stems accumulate at the center, but this isn't anything to get excited about. Merely prune and trim. Plants benefit greatly by a good dousing of water spray occasionally and do require shady moist conditions. Insects and diseases are rarely problems, but good humidity is a must.

DAVALLIAS

These are lacy Ferns, delicately beautiful, and grow with a hairy rhizome scanning the soil. Don't bury the rhizome in soil or it will cause rot. Although lovely, Davallias are prone to scale attack and finicky about watering. If soil becomes too dry, they wilt and rarely recover.

ADIANTUMS

These include the lovely maidenhair ferns. Although beautiful, they're touchy plants that resent drafts or bad conditions. Although not normally subject to insect attack, weak plants will have their troubles.

POLYPODIUMS

These are favorites, yet I'll never know why. They have large fronds that overlap each other and thus can't get good ventilation. Plants invariably are prone to fungus when they're grown so lush, and scale especially likes Polypodiums.

PLATYCERIUMS

These are actually epiphytic plants that require growing on cork or moss bark and not in a pot because in soil they generally perish in a short time. On bark they require loads of water and misting or leaves turn brown at the edges.

Note: Lately nurseries have started selling outdoor Ferns in their zeal to supply plants to the public. Ask specifically because an outdoor fern will not succeed indoors. Generally avoid overfeeding any Fern: excess salts can become toxic.

Ficus

A varied group including some easy and some difficult ones. *Ficus benjamina,* the banyan tree, loses most of its leaves once a year, so be prepared and don't panic. Other Ficus, such as the rubber tree, are impervious or almost so to insects, but the fiddleleaf fig (*Ficus lyrata*) has its problems: lower leaves drop. Sometimes this is virus, other times it's simply drafts or overheating. Touchy plants in general, with a few exceptions.

Geraniums

It seems that Geraniums are more prone to disease problems than insects. Aphids and mealybugs, as usual, lead the insect list, and occasionally red spider may attack a plant. Generally, however, if kept cool and grown under proper conditions, Geraniums are trouble-free.

Of the diseases, bacterial leaf spot and stem rot are most likely to occur. Cure is difficult, so sometimes it's better to discard the plant. Botrytis blight may occur, but if soil is kept free of dead or decaying leaves, it can be avoided. Edema—a condition caused by overwatering—is common with ivy-leaved Geraniums. It is really a cultural problem, not a disease. Verticillium wilt, a rare problem, happens only if you've used infected soil.

Gesneriads

This group includes African violets, Kohlerias, Episcias, Aesychnanthus, and Columneas. You'll have to be a very, very good gardener to keep these plants healthy. They have restricting requirements, and nobody is perfect, so eventually plants become attacked by insects or by disease. If you grow these lovely beauties, be on the watch for mealybugs, red spider, and fungus ailments, and you'll be constantly referring to Chapters 3 and 4 in this book. At present, this is a popular group of plants for the artificial-light garden.

Kalanchoe

I wish there were a good common name for this group of houseplants, because then perhaps they would be grown more. Generally, *Kalanchoe blossfeldiana* or one of its varieties is what you will get from the florist. These are such handsome plants, I suggest them even though they are subject to mealybugs, but you can avoid the pests by keeping the plants in well-ventilated places and being sure there are no bacterial infections (which also bother Kalanchoes). Try to keep water off the leaves. Otherwise,

I like these, and I think you will too because they *do bloom indoors* and offer great color in winter.

Kangaroo Vine, Grape Ivy (Cissus)

From the Grape family, these are fine performers and make a great show. Occasionally red spider may attack, but otherwise the plants seem to grow and grow without complaint. Highly recommended for beginners. A major step to a healthy Cissus is the method of spraying leaves frequently with water to keep them free of pests. Because grape ivies grow so quickly, many times if I see some red-spider damage on leaves, I clip off the stem rather than resort to chemicals in the home. I suggest you do the same. It makes the plant grow more vigorously.

Orchids

A large group of fine indoor plants including Cattleyas, Cypripediums and Phalaenopses. The Cattleyas and Phalaenopses have tough leathery leaves that are rarely attacked by any insect. Cypripediums with softer leaves occasionally get mealybug. While Orchid plants are rarely attacked by insects, flower buds many times are victims of thrips or aphids. Ants contribute to the aphid problem by transporting the critters to the buds so if you see ants on your plants, beware!

Occasionally, orchids are subject to disease or a virus but this is usually because of bad cultural practices and there are remedies to combat these problems, but it is a tricky procedure and requires a specialist or at least a good book on orchids.

Palms

Many fine plants here, and most are trouble-free, including: fishtail palm, bamboo palm, sentry palm, and lady palm. Palms rarely have any trouble if you keep fronds washed with a damp cloth. Occasionally the bamboo palm will drop lower leaves, but this is natural. If you buy the large sentry palms, be careful because they're exorbitant in price and not all are true to type. There *are* pygmy varieties that look like their big cousins but never grow over 36 inches. Lately, *Phoenix roebelinii,* the date palm, has become popular with decorators. Buy it at an outdoor nursery where it will cost less than through a plant shop. Actually, this is an outdoor plant, but seems to make the transition to indoors without too much trouble.

Peperomias and Pileas

These plants are so frequently used as terrarium subjects that they are listed here together. Most Peperomias and Pileas are small and ideally suited to closed-case growing. In all my years of growing these plants (and it has been many) I have never had any insects bother them. They seem almost invincible and thus, I am speechless or wordless so this paragraph is short.

Philodendrons

A favorite group and fine for low-light areas. The main concern with Philodendrons is that leaves get smaller as plant gets bigger, and no wonder. Most Philodendrons are viners, and for the young leaves to reach maturity they must gather moisture from aerial roots. Usually these aerial roots are left flopping in the air, but they should be tied to a wooden stake or bark support kept moist; then you'll get natural, big leaves, the way it should be.

No specific favorites here because there are so many good ones, and generally plants are rarely troubled with insects or disease. Red spider will occasionally bother a very dried out plant, but otherwise you're home free with these plants.

Note: Philodendrons, unlike many plants, will tolerate some drafts without wilting.

Spider Plant (Chlorophytum)

Rarely bothered by anything and can even get along without water for weeks because they have their own water reservoirs, as evidenced by swollen roots. You can't go wrong with this. And as the little plantlets grow, be sure to propagate a few of them and you will have spider plants forever!

Swedish Ivy (Plectranthus)

Another popular basket plant, and rightly so. It grows quickly and lushly, even in dim corners, and is a robust plant, rarely troubled. Occasionally, if conditions are too dry, some mealybugs might attack. Otherwise, sit back and show off this fine plant. Recently a variegated Swedish ivy has appeared, which is somewhat more temperamental than the standard type, and a small-leaved, furry variety is still another choice. This latter plant has a somewhat odd scent and is more susceptible to drafts and fluctuating temperatures than the others. This always makes me wary, for then the plant becomes weakened and may be subject to fungus attack.

Wandering Jew (Tradescantia, Zebrina)

The popular Wandering Jew is a favorite basket plant. In the past, only one variety was available, now there are all kinds of wandering Jews, some tricolor, others almost red in color, still others green and white, and so on. Tradescantias and Zebrinas are trouble-free plants. If they have any problems, it's because they grow too fast too much.

I believe some cutting and trimming is absolutely necessary or the plant becomes a tangle of closely grown leaves that thwart ventilation and set up circumstances for bacterial problems. Besides, trimming will give you a better-looking plant, so don't be afraid to wield the knife.

In their natural habitat, these plants grow as delicate vines on the ground. When they are brought indoors and planted in hanging baskets, the individual trailers tend to lose their oldest leaves, toward the base of the plant. These will turn brown, and no encouragement or "pinching back" will help to create new growth at the base of the stalk. Instead, the plant sends out new trailers and thus it should stay full and attractive, replenishing itself. If not, take cuttings as you trim the ends of the plant, and root them back into the pot.